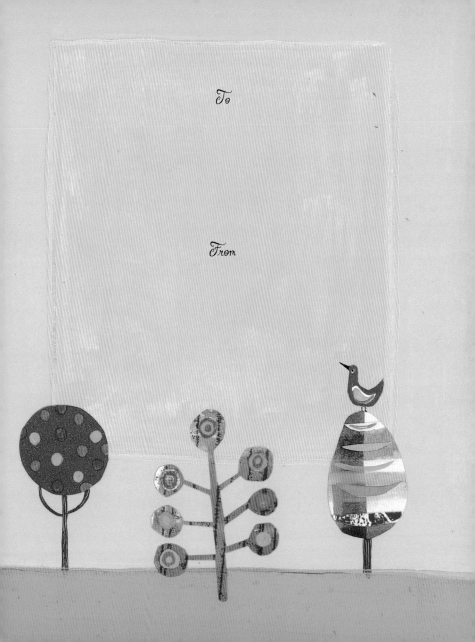

To

From

Prayers for Each and Every Day

2008 First Printing this edition

Written and compiled by Sophie Piper
Illustrations copyright © 2008 Anne Wilson
This edition copyright © 2008 Lion Hudson

The moral rights of the author and illustrator
have been asserted

Published in the United States by Paraclete Press, 2008.
ISBN: 978-1-55725-622-5
Originally published in 2008 by Lion Hudson plc
Wilkinson House, Jordan Hill Road,
Oxford OX2 8DR, England
www.lionhudson.com
ISBN: 978 0 7459 6014 2

1 3 5 7 9 10 8 6 4 2 0

Acknowledgments

All unattributed prayers are by Sophie Piper, copyright © Lion Hudson.

Prayers by Lois Rock are copyright © Lion Hudson.

Bible extracts are taken or adapted from the Good News Bible,
published by The Bible Societies/HarperCollins Publishers Ltd, UK
© American Bible Society 1966, 1971, 1976, 1992, used by permission.

The Lord's Prayer (on page 9) from Common Worship: Services
and Prayers for the Church of England (Church House Publishing, 2000)
is copyright © The English Language Liturgical Consultation, 1988
and is reproduced by permission of the publishers.

Published by Paraclete Press
Brewster, Massachusetts
www.paracletepress.com

Printed and bound in China

Prayers for Each and Every Day

Sophie Piper

Illustrated by Anne Wilson

PARACLETE PRESS

BREWSTER, MASSACHUSETTS

Contents

When You Pray

To pray is to spend time with God. It is to stand in the presence of love itself and to set one's heart on living in the way that is right and good.

This book can help you learn to pray. There is a page of prayers for every day of the week, both morning and evening.

There are also prayers for special days and special times.

As well as saying these prayers, you can use your own words to talk to God about the things that matter to you.

As you pray, remember these words of Jesus:

'Ask, and you will receive; seek, and you will find; knock, and the door will be opened to you.

'Your Father in heaven will give good things to those who ask him.'

From Matthew 7:7, 11

A Prayer for
Every Day

When Jesus lived on earth, his friends and followers asked him to teach them how to pray. Here is what he taught them to say. You can say these words every time you come to pray.

Our Father in heaven,
hallowed be your name,
your kingdom come,
your will be done,
on earth as in heaven.
Give us today our daily bread.
Forgive us our sins
as we forgive those who sin against us.
Lead us not into temptation
but deliver us from evil.
Amen

The Lord's Prayer

Monday Morning

Day by day,
dear Lord, of thee
three things I pray:
to see thee more clearly,
love thee more dearly,
follow thee more nearly,
day by day.

Richard of Chichester
(1197–1253)

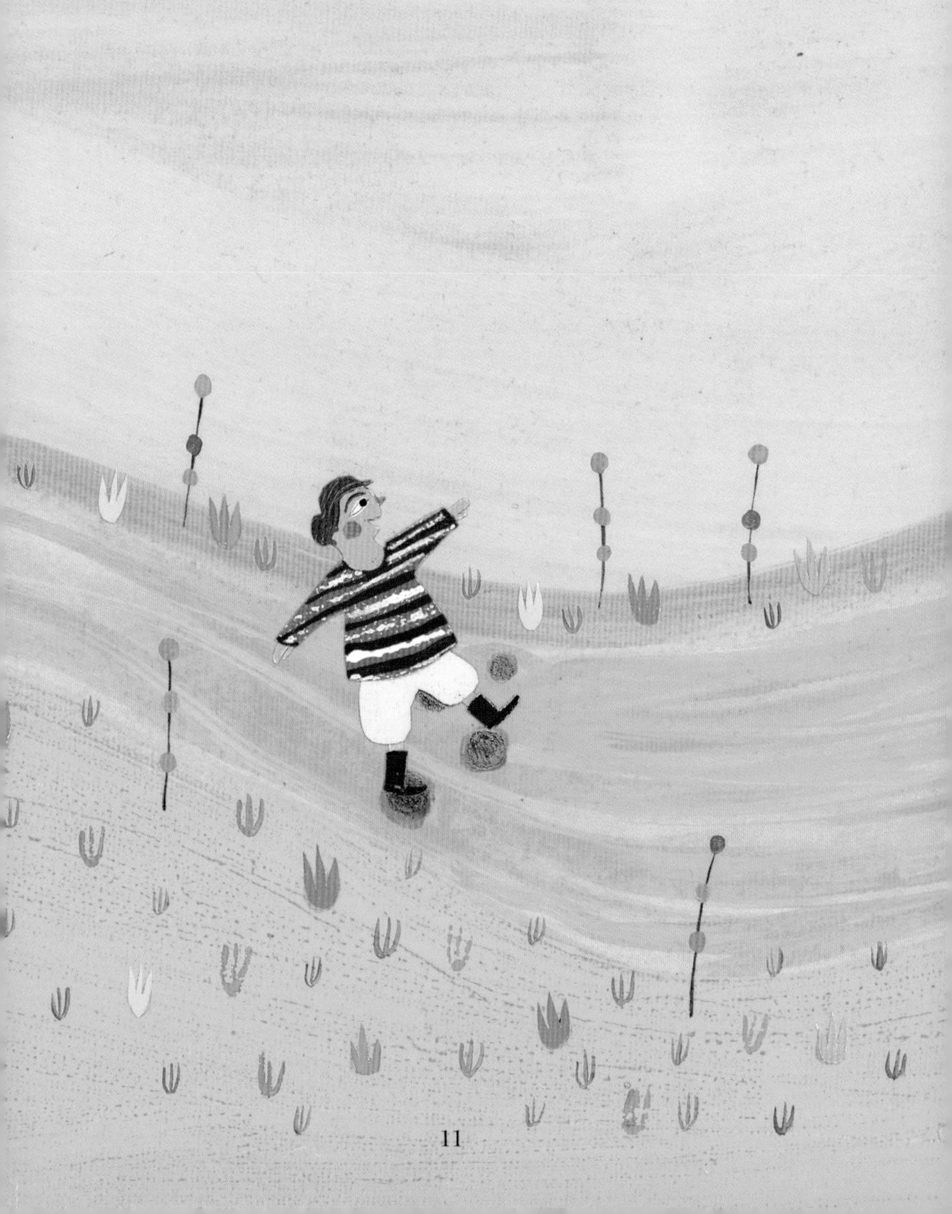

Monday Evening

Jesus told this story:

'A man went out to sow. As he scattered the seed, some of it fell along the path. Birds swooped down and ate it up. Some of it fell on rocky ground. The seedlings sprouted quickly, only to wilt in the dry soil. Some of the seed fell among thorn bushes. They grew up with the plants and choked them.

'But some of the seed fell in good soil; the plants grew and produced corn, a hundred grains each.'

Jesus went on to explain the meaning:

'The seed is the word of God. The seeds on the path stand for those who hear the word only to have the Devil come and snatch it away. The seeds that fell on rocky ground stand for those who welcome God's message but do not have faith enough to last when times are hard. The seeds that fell among thorn bushes stand for those who hear God's word but who let everyday things crowd in and choke their faith.

'The seeds that fell in good soil stand for those who hear the message and obey it. They stay faithful to God, and their lives bear fruit.'

From Luke 8:5–15

Tuesday Morning

Jesus said this:

'Look at the wild birds and how God provides them with the food they need.

'Look at the wild flowers and how wonderfully God clothes them for their brief day in the sun.

'If God takes this much care of the birds and the flowers, you can be sure God will take care of you.'

From Matthew 6:26–30

Dear God,
May I be fair to others
and make this world a better place.
If I see someone being treated unfairly,
may I go to help them.
If I see someone in need,
may I share with them what I have.
For I believe that you will bless me.
I believe that your goodness will shine on me
like the morning sun.

From Isaiah 58:6–8

Tuesday Evening

God will bless those
   who do what is right,
      those who say no to wrongdoing.
      They will be like trees that grow
      beside a stream,
         that stay green in the driest
         summer
         and bear rich fruit at harvest
         time:
         everything they do will go
         well.

From Psalm 1

God will bless poor people:
the kingdom of God belongs to them.
God will bless those who go hungry:
God will fill them with good things.
God will bless those who weep for sadness:
God will make them laugh for joy.
God will bless those who are bullied and laughed at
as they try to do what is right:
they can be happy inside, knowing that they will have
a great reward in heaven.

From Luke 6:20–23

Wednesday Morning

Dear God, help me to forgive others just as I want them to forgive me.

From Matthew 6:14

From the mud
a pure white flower

From the storm
a clear blue sky

As we pardon
one another

God forgives us
from on high.

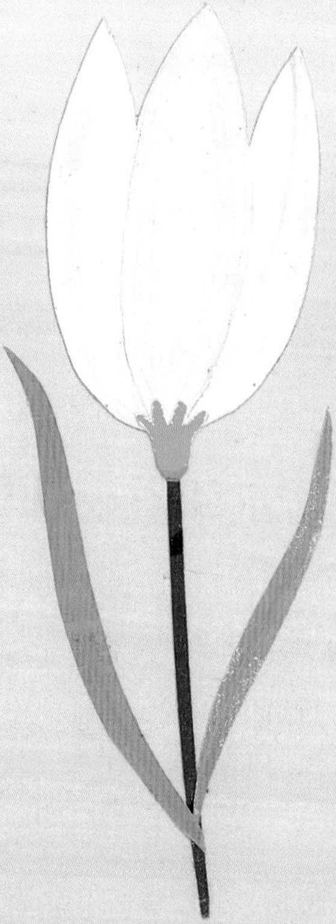

Wednesday Evening

I told God everything:
I told God about all the wrong things I had
done.
I gave up trying to pretend.
I gave up trying to hide.
I knew that the only thing to do was to confess.

And God forgave me.

From Psalm 32:5

Take my wrongdoing and throw it away,
down in the deep of the sea;
welcome me into your kingdom of love
for all of eternity.

From Micah 7:18–20

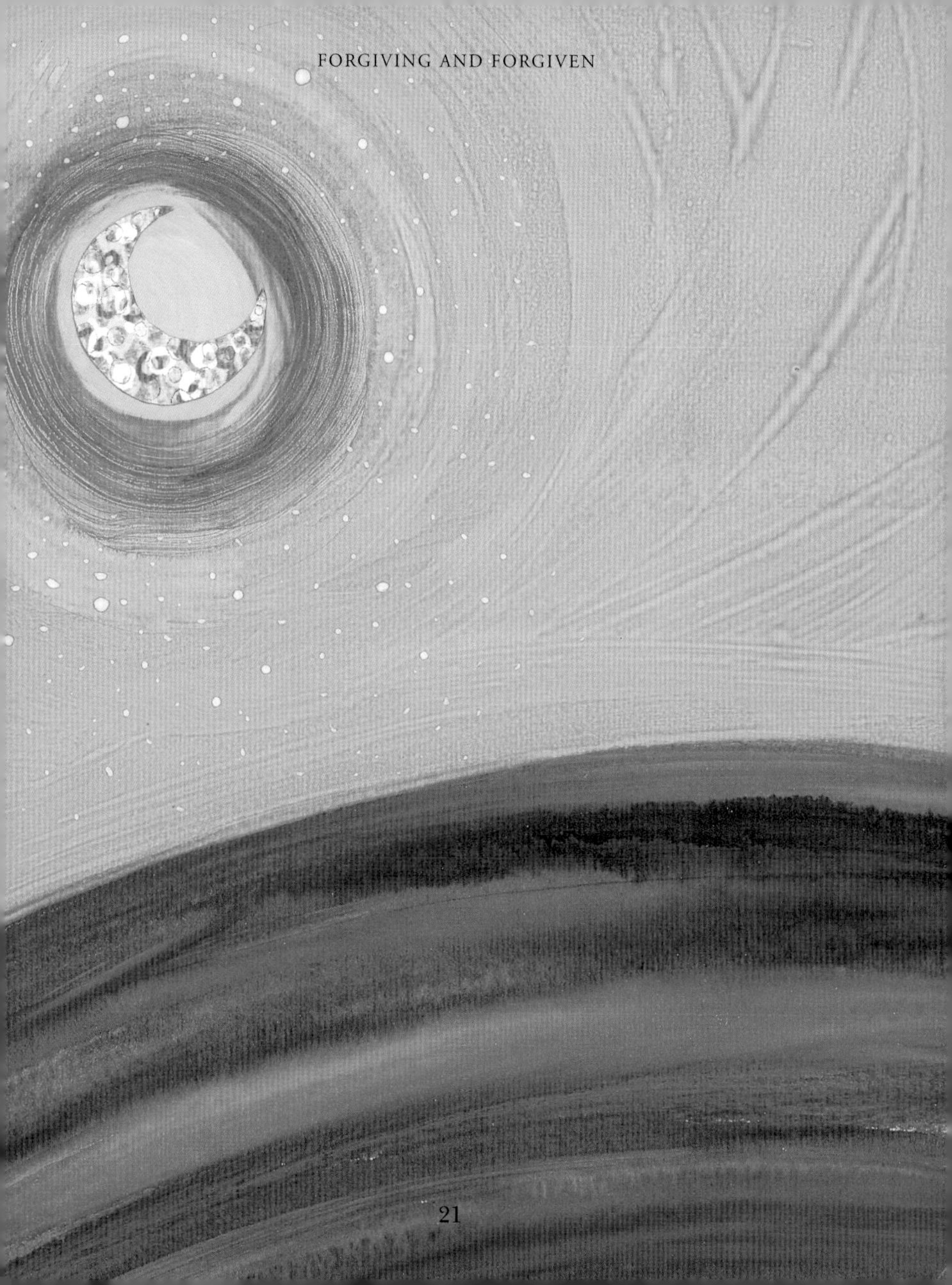

Thursday Morning

Jesus told this story:

'There was once a man who had two sons. He went to the elder and said, "Please go and work in the vineyard today."

'"I don't want to," came the sullen reply.

'The father went to his other son and asked the same thing.

'"Yes, father, of course," the young man answered cheerfully.

'Later the elder felt sorry for what he had said. He went to the vineyard and worked all day. The younger simply lazed around.

'Now ask yourself,' said Jesus, 'which of the two did what his father wanted?'

From Matthew 21:28–31

Thursday Evening

Spirit of God
put love in my life.

Spirit of God
put joy in my life.

Spirit of God
put peace in my life.

Spirit of God
make me patient.

Spirit of God
make me kind.

Spirit of God
make me good.

Spirit of God
give me faithfulness.

Spirit of God
give me humility.

Spirit of God
give me self-control.

From Galatians 5:22–23

Friday Morning

Lord Jesus,
Make me as kind to others
as I would want to be to you.

Make me as generous to others
as I would want to be to you.

May I take time to help them
as I would take time to help you.

May I take the trouble to help them
as I would take the trouble to help you.

May I look into the faces of those I meet
and see your face.

From Matthew 25:37–40

Jesus said this:

'Love the people who don't like you; pray for those people who are unkind to you. You are to be good to them just as God is good to them. For God gives the sun and rain to bad people as well as good people.'

From Matthew 5:44–45

Friday Evening

Dear friends, let us love one another, because love comes from God.

1 John 4:7–11

Help me, Lord, to show your love.

Help me to be patient and kind, not jealous or conceited or proud. May I never be ill-mannered, selfish or irritable; may I be quick to forgive and forget.

May I not gloat over wrongdoing, but rather be glad about things that are good and true.

May I never give up loving: may my faith and hope and patience never come to an end.

From 1 Corinthians 13:4–7

Love is giving, not taking,
mending, not breaking,
trusting, believing,
never deceiving,
patiently bearing
and faithfully sharing
each joy, every sorrow,
today and tomorrow.

Anonymous

Saturday Morning

May all the world sing to our God!
The angels in the heights,
the sun, the moon, the silver stars
that glitter in the night;

The ocean and the giant whales,
the storms and wind and rain,
the animals and birds on every
mountain, hill and plain;

And all the people, young and old,
the wealthy and the poor:
sing praise to God who made the world,
sing praise for evermore!

From Psalm 148

Saturday Evening

God's own peace to the mountain,
God's own peace to the plain:
God's own Paradise garden
Grow in the world again.

Lois Rock

O God, your greatness is seen in all the world!

I look at the sky, which you have made; at the moon and the stars, which you set in their places, and I wonder:

Who am I, that you think of me?

What is humankind, that you care for us?

O God, your greatness is seen in all the world!

From Psalm 8:1, 3–4

Sunday Morning

Dear God,
Help me to grow up good.

Help me not to make mistakes just because
I am young.

Help me to be righteous without being smug;
faithful to you without being narrow-minded;
loving without being naïve;
peaceable without being weak.

Help me, dear God, because I ask you.

From 2 Timothy 2:22

Thank you, kind God, for your day of rest.

May we spend its hours on things that bring honour to you and joy to us all.

Sunday Evening

God is wise and loves you with wisdom.
God is good and loves you with goodness.
God is holy and loves you with holiness.
God is just and loves you with justice.
God is merciful and loves you with mercy.
God is kind and loves you with kindness.
God is gentle and loves you with gentleness.

From St John of the Cross (1542–91)

O God,
as truly as you are our father,
so just as truly you are our mother.
We thank you, God our father,
for your strength and goodness.
We thank you, God our mother,
for the closeness of your caring.
O God, we thank you for the great love
you have for each one of us.

Julian of Norwich (1342–c.1416)

God is my light and my salvation;
I will fear no one.

God protects me from all danger;
I will never be afraid.

From Psalm 27:1

The Christian Year

The Christian year is a pattern of festivals, and each one shines a light on a different part of the Christian faith.

Here are prayers to guide you through the Christian year.

Dear God,
My faith is no bigger than a seed.
Let it grow into a tree.

Lois Rock

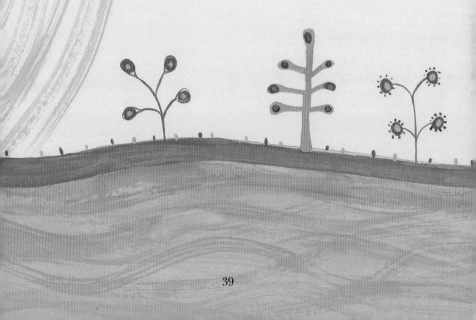

Advent

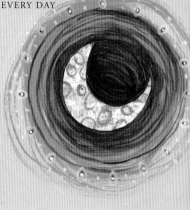

In the dark hours
I wait for morning light.

In the cold hours
I wait for warming sun.

In the sad hours
I wait for the return of joy

and a Christmas feeling
that will last for always.

Christmas

Let us travel to Christmas
By the light of a star.
Let us go to the hillside
Right where the shepherds are.
Let us see shining angels
Singing from heaven above.
Let us see Mary cradling
God's holy child with love.

Lois Rock

Epiphany

The wise men read the skies above,
and now we read their story
of how they found the prince of peace,
newborn from heaven's glory.

We come, as if to Bethlehem,
to offer gifts of love
to make this world at Christmas time
a piece of heaven above.

Lois Rock

Lent

Lent is a time
for giving up something valuable
so we can remember
how great a blessing it is to us.

Lent is a time
for taking up something valuable
so we can remember
to bring some blessing to others.

Lois Rock

Palm Sunday

We sing and clap and wave and cheer
for Jesus, who comes riding near.

We cheer and wave and clap and sing
to welcome Jesus as our king.

Lois Rock

May the words I speak
tell others of Jesus.

May the things I do
tell others of Jesus.

May my whole life
tell others of Jesus.

From the letter of James

The Last Supper

Jesus' body,
Broken bread,
By God's word
We all are fed.

Jesus' lifeblood,
Wine that's spilt,
As one temple
We are built.

At this table
Take your place:
Feast upon
God's love and grace.

Lois Rock

Good Friday

Jesus said a prayer for his enemies:

'Forgive them, Father! They don't know what they are doing.'

From Luke 23:34

I will walk with Jesus.
– But you may be betrayed.
I will walk with Jesus.
– But you may be abandoned.
I will walk with Jesus.
– But you may be given a cross too heavy to bear.
I will walk with Jesus.
– But you cannot know where that may lead.
I will walk with Jesus.
– Then may Jesus walk with you through life
  and through death.

Lois Rock

Easter

Very early on Sunday morning, the women went to the tomb. They found the stone rolled away and the tomb empty. Suddenly two figures in bright shining clothes stood by them saying, 'Why are you looking among the dead for one who is alive? He is not here; he has been raised to life.'

From Luke 24

The tree of thorns
is dressed in bloom
for resurrection day;
and joy springs from
the underworld
now death is put away.

Lois Rock

Ascension and Pentecost

Christ has no body now on earth but yours,
no hands but yours, no feet but yours…
Yours are the feet with which he is to go about doing good,
and yours are the hands with which he is to bless us now.

St Teresa of Avila (1515–82)

Let the Spirit come
like the winds that blow:
take away my doubts;
help my faith to grow.

Let the Spirit come
like a flame of gold:
warm my heart within;
make me strong and bold.

Lois Rock

Harvest Thanksgiving

Dear God,
Thank you
for being so good to us.
Thank you
for listening to our prayers.
Thank you
for the world we live in:
the summer and the winter,
the sunshine and the rain;
the time for sowing seeds
and the time to gather crops.
Thank you for all the good things
the world gives us.

From Psalm 65

The harvests have ripened in the sun;
There's plenty of food for everyone:
There's some for ourselves
   and more to share
With all of God's people everywhere.

Lois Rock

Each time we eat,
may we remember God's love.

Prayer from China

In Times of Need

O God,
be to me
like the evergreen tree
and shelter me in your shade,
and bless me again
like the warm gentle rain
that gives life to all you have made.

From Hosea 14:4–8

Thank you, God, that you help us in our troubles, so that we can help others who have all kinds of troubles.

From 2 Corinthians 1:4

Blessings

May the Lord bless you,
may the Lord take care of you;
May the Lord be kind to you,
may the Lord be gracious to you;
May the Lord look on you with favour,
may the Lord give you peace.

From Numbers 6:24–26

Index of First Lines of Prayers